GEORGE FRIDERIC HANDEL

MUSIC FOR THE ROYAL FIREWORKS

HWV 351

Edited by/Herausgegeben von
Roger Fiske

T0081234

Ernst Eulenburg Ltd

London · Mainz · Madrid · New York · Paris · Prague · Tokyo · Toronto · Zürich

CONTENTS

Performance material based on this edition is available from the publisher/
Der hier veröffentlichte Notentext ist auch als Aufführungsmaterial beim Verlag erhältlich/
Le matériel d'exécution réalisé à partir de cette édition est disponible auprès de l'éditeur

Eulenburg Orchestral Series: EOS 1307

Ernst Eulenburg Ltd
48 Great Marlborough Street
London W1F 7BB

PREFACE

The War of the Austrian Succession officially ended with the signing of the Peace of Aix-la-Chapelle on 7 October 1748, and celebrations, postponed until reasonable weather might be expected, were planned in London for 27 April 1749. During the winter an elaborate pavilion was built in Green Park from which royalty and lesser notables could see the fireworks and hear Handel's music. Fireworks experts from Italy were engaged. On 28 March the Duke of Monmouth wrote as follows to the Comptroller of His Majesty's Fireworks:

Hendel now proposes to have but 12 trumpets and 12 French horns; at first there was to have been sixteen of each, and I remember I told the King so, who, at that time, objected to there being any musick; but, when I told him the quantity and number of martial musick there was to be, he was better satisfied, and said he hoped there would be no fidles. Now Hendel proposes to lessen the nomber of trumpets, &c. and to have violeens. I dont at all doubt but when the King hears it he will be very much displeased. If the thing war to be in such a manner as certainly to please the King, it ought to consist of no kind of instrument but martial instruments.[1]

Jonathan Tyers, proprietor of Vauxhall Gardens, offered to lend for the occasion 'all his lanterns, lamps, &c. to the value of seven hundred pounds' and 30 of his men to put them up, on condition that Handel's music was rehearsed at Vauxhall. Handel opposed this suggestion but was over-ruled; the saving of money was irresistible. By now he had come down to 9 trumpets and 9 horns, together with 24 oboes, 12 bassoons, one double bassoon and perhaps a serpent, 3 pairs of kettle drums and 2(?) side drums – at least 60 players in all. He wrote these numbers on his score to ensure that enough parts were copied.

The rehearsal in Vauxhall Gardens took place on 21 April at 11.00 a.m., and according to *The Gentleman's Magazine* 12,000 people paid half-a-crown to get in. 'So great a resort occasioned such a stoppage on London Bridge, that no carriage could pass for 3 hours', even though Westminster Bridge was also available and much nearer. In Green Park the music began soon after 6 o'clock and then came the fireworks; there is no evidence that they coincided. When part of the pavilion was set on fire, 'the Chevalier Servandoni, who designed the building, drawing his sword and affronting […] the Comptroller of the Ordnance and Fireworks, he was disarmed and taken into custody, but discharg'd the next day on asking pardon.'

Handel's Autograph MS

Handel's autograph score in the British Library's Royal Music Collection (*GB-Lbl* RM20.g.7) is the only important source. It is a very confusing one because after the Green Park performance (or just possibly before it) Handel added string parts, in most cases by the simple expedient of making the strings double the wind. At the same time he added instructions for the repeating of certain pieces with different instrumentation, but it is hard to tell if these instructions refer to performances with strings or without. A comparison of previous editions of the final Minuet will give some indication of the difficulty of achieving an Urtext. Chrysander set it out on 10 staves with Corno 1 and 2 both doubling Tromba 2. The previous Eulenburg edition has 11 staves and Corno 1 doubling Tromba 1; both this score and Chrysander's include Handel's directions for repeats but neither makes clear what instruments should play the first time because Handel himself never made this clear. A similar confusion afflicts *La Réjouissance*. Full details are given in the Editorial Notes below.

Handel was in the middle of *La Réjouissance* before he thought of adding strings. He went back to the beginning of his score and wrote 'e Violino I' etc. under the first bars of the relevant

[1] Quoted in Otto Erich Deutsch, *Handel, a Documentary Biography* (London, 1955), 661

staves, and in the margin of the *Bourrée* he added V.1 and V.2 above the centrally-placed H.1 and H.2[2]; the alignment shows that these string directions were afterthoughts and this is also the case with *La Paix*. But in the Minuet that follows *La Réjouissance* the violin indications are exactly opposite the staves and not afterthoughts, and there were originally four string staves in the final Minuet. To add to the confusion most of the string staves and doubling indications in the later pieces have been lightly crossed out, probably, but not certainly, by Handel himself. There is also a line through the words under the *Bourrée*, 'La seconda volta senza Hautb. e Bassons', which are themselves an implication of strings in this piece. Why should Handel seemingly decide to have strings and then decide not to have them?

The Gentleman's Magazine for April reported 100 players at Vauxhall, and it has been argued that this proves Handel had his way about including strings, but it is improbable that he would have gone against the King's wishes, and those who reported a band of 100 are more likely to have guessed the number than counted the players. Furthermore the most convincing explanation of the crossings-out is that Handel did not want his Green Park copyists to waste their limited time on string parts which would not be wanted. While writing *La Réjouissance* he had come to realize that his music would have no subsequent performances unless string parts were included, so he began to include them. But he kept his crossings-out light in order not to conceal what Walsh would subsequently publish for more modest indoor performances; the first of these was at the Foundling Hospital in London on 27 May. Perhaps he did not cross out the doubling indications in the earlier pieces because he did not add them until the Green Park celebrations were over.

As well as the afterthoughts he wrote with some care Handel later added others with no care at all. '2 fois' over the *Bourrée* and first Minuet and 'the third time all together' under *La Réjouissance* were scribbled very hurriedly indeed. *GB-Lbl* RM20.g.7 also includes two concertos whose resemblance to the *Fireworks Music* has sometimes been exaggerated. In each the slow introduction is very like the somewhat longer one in the Ouverture, but other resemblances are minimal. The Concerto in F is scored for oboes, bassoons, 4 horns and strings, begins with two horns on their own and has only two movements. The other concerto is in D because Handel wanted to add trumpets and drums which could not then be played in F. He also added a fugue in the middle:

This subject derives from the *Fireworks Ouverture* bb99–102. The brief likeness between b48 in the *Ouverture* (woodwind) and b1 of the Concerto finales (but no dotted rhythm here) is surely coincidental.

Published editions

Walsh was quick to publish the *Fireworks Music* 'in all its Parts, viz. French Horns, Trumpets, Kettle Drums, Violins, Hoboys, Violoncello, & Bassoons. with a Thorough Bass for the Harpsichord or Organ'. He did not include a viola part. Also he ignored the 'Basson I' stave in the *Ouverture*, and made no mention of the Contra Bassoon or Side Drum. One part is labelled 'Hautboy & Violino I', another 'Hautboy & Violino II'; Hautboy III doubles Hautboy II in the later pieces, and the 'Basson e C. Basso e Violoncello' part is figured. Thus the string and woodwind parts are identical throughout.

A 2-stave arrangement for the 'German Flute, Violin or Harpsichord' also appeared, and this could be played in the home either as a keyboard solo or by a melody instrument with continuo accompaniment (the lower stave is figured). At the end Walsh added seven D major Marches

---

[2] For Hautboy or Oboe

(including 'See, the conquering Hero comes', the Marches in *The Occasional Oratorio* and *Samson*, and the Dead March in *Saul*) and an arrangement of the Coronation Anthem, *Zadok the Priest*. There is no evidence that these additions were played in Green Park.

Editorial Notes

AUT Handel's Autograph Full Score (*GB-Lbl* RM20.g.7)

PP   The Published Parts (Walsh, early June 1749)

Hps The arrangement for Harpsichord, etc. (Walsh, late July 1749)

HG *Händelgesellschaft*, Vol. 47, edited by Friedrich Chrysander

This present Eulenburg edition is based on AUT. Handel's verbal instructions are unaltered even when, as at the end, they are in three different languages. I have changed Hautb. and H.1 to Oboe and Ob.1, and Principale in the soprano clef to Tromba III in the treble clef; PP also made this latter change. The Principale was the military trumpet playing in the lower register as opposed to the Clarino playing in the higher one; as in the *Dettingen Te Deum* Handel limited it almost entirely to arpeggio notes.

In the *Bourrée* Handel wrote 'Viola colli Bassi', and bar 2 note 4 suggests he meant loco, but if so the violas must jump up an octave from b5 n2. Should they stay there for the rest of the piece? In *La Réjouissance* Chrysander saw 'e Viola' against the Tromba III stave and decided that they should double an octave below, but just before the repeat marks this results in notes Handel cannot possibly have meant, though they appear in HG and many later editions. It is not surprising that Walsh should never have published a viola part. The viola part that is issued with the material based on this edition follows Handel's doubling directions except when they take the instrument out of its 18th-century compass. In Handel's day violists adjusted in similar fashion on their own initiative.

As in the D major Suite in the *Water Music* there are no dynamics. In Green Park every instrument will have played fortissimo, dynamic

contrasts arising from contrasts in the orchestration.

Editorial markings: editorial additions are placed within square brackets. Editorial slurs or ties are shown as broken lines.

Ouverture

The title shows Handel wanted it played in the French style with double-dotting. AUT has 'Concerto Adagio' crossed out; the similar slow introductions in the two concertos are both marked Largo. Handel had previously written for a double bassoon in *L'Allegro* (1740); he added 'Serpent' after Contra Bassone but later crossed it out – not necessarily before the first performance.

24   VIII, nn3–4: even quavers in HG and later editions; dotted rhythm in AUT and PP.

44–46 above these bars Handel crossed out four words leaving the second illegible: 'Alla … de Guerre'.

62   Cor 3, n3: e' in AUT and PP but this note was then virtually unplayable and taking it for an error I have put it up an octave.

88   Tr 3, n3: wrongly given in HG and later editions as b', then unplayable on the trumpet. After making some messy alterations Handel wrote this note on the second line from the top, forgetting that with his Principale in the soprano clef the result would be b', but he showed what he meant by writing the letter d above the note. PP has d" which is certainly right. (Handel also mistook his Tromba 3 stave in bb25 and 42.)

101, 164 Ob1/VII, nn4–6: as in AUT. In 101 PP has Ob1 in the rhythm of Ob2, but in 164 prefers the dotted rhythm for Ob1.

111–114 these bars were a later addition, squashed in at the end of one page and the beginning of another.

176   HG and later editions have unbarred C as in PP, but AUT clearly shows a

barred C, which may imply a faster tempo than at the start of the movement.

Bourrée

(*Bourée* in Aut, PP, and Hps)
Originally for woodwind only; the numbers show that Ob2/3 both play the middle stave; PP confirms this. '2 fois' and the words at the bottom were late additions, perhaps only relevant when there were strings. PP has 'twice' but without suggesting a different instrumentation.

25   Ob1, n1: g" in HG and more recent editions but AUT has a" which is certainly right: PP intended a" but deceived by omitting the leger line.

La Paix

Staves 4 and 5 originally labelled H1 and H2 (i.e. oboes). Handel later wrote 'Tr e Vl' on top but without obliterating the H; similarly for stave 5. Tr cannot mean trumpets (as in one modern score) because they could not have played the notes; it must mean *flauto traverso*, an instrument not otherwise mentioned in AUT. Perhaps there were flutes at the Foundling Hospital performance.

1, 2   Ob1: PP, Hps, HG and later editions all slur nn4–6 (similarly Ob2 in b1), but the slurs in AUT clearly cover only nn4–5.

14   Cor1, nn4–5: HG and later editions have even quavers, but AUT and PP show the same dotted rhythm as for Ob1.

La Réjouissance

Originally Handel seems to have begun with trumpets and drums only, and later (before the Green Park performance?) asked for a repeat by woodwind and horns, but there is no indication of these instruments in the margin at the start, apart from 'et Hautb' hastily scribbled under b1 of the Tromba 1 stave as a late afterthought. At b11 Handel happened to be starting a new system with 2 staves to spare, and with an eye to the future he used one for the two violins and the other for the violas. Also from b5 he added notes for VlII to the Tromba 2 stave; this made possible much-needed C sharps which the trumpets could not play. There was space at the foot of the previous page so he then added a 'Violoncelli e Contra Bassi' stave in bb1–4 (the barlines are not linked to those in the staves above – evidence that the stave was an afterthought) and doubling indications for the upper strings. Later still he crossed these out (except for VlII) as also the viola stave from b11. PP: 'First time with Trumpets, Second time with French Horns, Third time Altogether', the implication being that at the Foundling Hospital the strings and woodwind played all three times, but this is not supported by AUT. The fact is that Handel never made his intentions clear.

9   VlII, n8: a' in PP, HG and later editions but AUT (hard to decipher here) seems to show F sharp which makes good sense.

10   Tr2, n7: PP, HG and later editions have d" which does not fit the harmony. AUT seems to show a' which does fit.

Menuet I.

Written across the top of 2 facing pages in AUT, leaving 9 blank staves below on each. With Handel this usually means the piece was added later; he never wasted paper if he could possibly avoid it. Perhaps he added this Minuet for the Foundling Hospital performance: it would not have been very effective out-of-doors (but the same might be said of the *Bourrée*). '2 fois' presumably applies only to performances with strings. PP: 'twice' but without indicating a different instrumentation. Presumably the woodwind play the first time, the strings the second. There is no evidence that Handel wanted this piece played as a Trio to the next one, but it may have been.

Menuet II.

AUT has 8 staves, the top 4 for trumpets and drums. The others were originally for strings but Handel wrote H1 and H2 on top of VII and

VIII (making them hard to read) and lightly crossed out the viola stave and the word 'Violoncelli' against the bottom one. He was surely adapting for Green Park a piece he had written on some previous occasion. His intentions as regards the first time round are not clear. PP, repeating the directions given for *La Réjouissance*, implies that strings and woodwind play all three times, but again AUT suggests otherwise. It is just possible that Handel wanted no strings in this piece even at the Foundling Hospital, in which case the woodwind play all three times, but strings and trumpets the first time seems more likely. Note that side drums are here in the plural.

5, 13　　the slurs may mean that Handel wanted these pairs of quavers played evenly, the others being treated as *notes inégales*.

Instrumental parts corresponding with this score are available from the publisher (Eulenburg Orchestral Series: EOS 1307). For conducting purposes, this score can be used. The gist of Handel's 2nd and 3rd time instructions are included in the parts (in English), but in practice conductors are not likely to play any piece three times with repeats (Handel may or may not have expected repeats the 2nd and 3rd times). A common solution is to apply his 2nd time instructions to the 1st time repeats, and then play the piece 'all together' without repeats. Thus in *La Réjouissance*:

{1st half: trumpets, drums (and strings?)
1st half: repeated by woodwind and horns only
{2nd half: trumpets, drums (and strings?)
2nd half: repeated by woodwind and horns only

The whole piece 'all together' means without repeats. Similarly in the final Minuet.

Handel's numbers show that in the *Ouverture* he wanted the Oboe 1 part emphasized, but in the later pieces he wanted the same number of oboists to each part. In performances with strings his intentions can best be realized with 6 oboists (3–2–1 in the *Ouverture*) or 4 (2–1–1 in the *Ouverture*). The bassoon parts should be doubled. Figures from PP and Hps bass line are omitted in this score and there are none in AUT; there cannot have been a harpsichord in Green Park and there is no necessity for one today.

Roger Fiske

VORWORT

Der österreichische Erbfolgekrieg endete offiziell am 7. Oktober 1748 mit der Unterzeichnung des Aachener Friedens. Die damit verbundenen Festlichkeiten, die vorerst verlegt wurden, um mit einigermaßen gutem Wetter rechnen zu können, waren für den 27. April 1749 in London geplant. Im Laufe des Winters wurde im Londoner Green Park ein kunstvoller Pavillon errichtet, von dem aus die Mitglieder der königlichen Familie sowie andere wichtige Persönlichkeiten das Feuerwerk sehen und Händels Musik hören konnten. Für diesen Anlass wurden Feuerwerksspezialisten aus Italien engagiert. Am 28. März schrieb der Herzog von Monmouth an den Kontrolleur der königlichen Feuerwerke:

Hendel [sic!] schlägt jetzt vor, nur 12 Trompeten und 12 Hörner zu benutzen; erst sollten es sechzehn von jeder Gattung sein, und ich erinnere mich daran, den König, der damals gar keine Musik haben wollte, davon unterrichtet zu haben. Als ich ihm jedoch sagte, wie viel Militärmusik dabei gespielt werden sollte, war er zufriedener und sagte, er hoffte, es wären keine Geigen dabei. Aber jetzt schlägt Hendel [sic!] vor, weniger Trompeten usw. zu benutzen und Geigen einzusetzen. Ich hege darüber keinen Zweifel, dass der König sehr ungehalten sein wird, wenn er davon hört. Wenn man die Sache so veranstalten will, dass sie dem König bestimmt gefällt, so sollten keine anderen Instrumente als Militärinstrumente verwendet werden.[1]

Der Besitzer der Vauxhall Gardens, Jonathan Tyers, bot für diese Gelegenheit „all seine Lampions, Laternen usw. im Wert von siebenhundert Pfund" an sowie dreißig seiner Leute, um sie aufzuhängen, allerdings unter der Bedingung, dass die Proben für Händels Musik in den Vauxhall Gardens stattfänden. Händel lehnte diesen Vorschlag ab, wurde aber überstimmt. Die dadurch mögliche Geldersparnis war zu verlockend. Inzwischen hatte er die Instrumentation auf neun Trompeten, neun Hörner, 24 Oboen, zwölf Fagotte, ein Kontrafagott und vielleicht ein Serpent, drei Paar Pauken und zwei (?) kleine Trommeln reduziert, was einer Besetzung von mindestens 60 Musikern entsprach. Er notierte diese Zahlen auf seiner Partitur, um sicherzustellen, dass die genügende Anzahl an Stimmen abgeschrieben wurde.

Die Probe in den Vauxhall Gardens fand am 21. April um 11 Uhr morgens statt, und laut *The Gentleman's Magazine* haben 12.000 Besucher je eine halbe Krone gezahlt, um bei diesem Ereignis dabei zu sein. „Ein derartig großes Ereignis führte zu einer solchen Verkehrsstockung auf der London Bridge, dass während eines Zeitraums von drei Stunden kein Wagen passieren konnte", obgleich die Westminster Bridge ebenfalls zur Verfügung stand und viel näher war. Im Green Park begann die Musik kurz nach 6 Uhr, darauf folgte das Feuerwerk; dass dies gleichzeitig stattfand, ist nicht belegt worden. Als ein Teil des Pavillons anfing zu brennen, „zog Chevalier Servandoni, der das Gebäude entworfen hatte, sein Schwert und griff [...] den Kontrolleur der Artillerie und des Feuerwerks an. Er wurde entwaffnet und in Verwahrung genommen, aber als er am nächsten Tag um Vergebung bat, wieder entlassen."

Händels Autograph

Händels Autograph der Partitur ist die einzige wesentliche Quelle. Es befindet sich in der Königlichen Musiksammlung der British Library (*GB-Lbl* RM20.g.7) und ist sehr verwirrend, da Händel nach der Aufführung im Green Park (oder kurz davor) Streicherstimmen hinzugefügt hat, wobei er die Streicher meist einfach die Bläserstimmen mitspielen ließ. Gleichzeitig fügte er Anweisungen hinzu, die angaben, dass die Wiederholungen bei gewissen Stücken mit veränderter Besetzung gespielt werden sollten. Es ist jedoch schwierig festzustellen, ob es sich dabei um Aufführungen mit oder ohne Streicher gehandelt hat. Ein Vergleich der verschiedenen

---

[1] Zitat aus Otto Erich Deutsch: *Handel. A Documentary Biography*, London 1955, S. 661.

früheren Ausgaben zeigt beispielsweise beim letzten Menuett, wie schwierig es ist, einen Urtext herzustellen. Chrysander hat für dieses Menuett zehn Notensysteme benutzt, wobei „Corno I und II" zusammen die Stimme der „Tromba II" spielen. Die vorige Eulenburg-Ausgabe hat elf Systeme, wobei „Corno I" die Stimme der „Tromba I" spielt. Diese Partitur und Chrysanders Partitur enthalten Händels Angaben bezüglich der Wiederholungen, aber in keiner von beiden wird erklärt, welche Instrumente beim ersten Mal spielen sollen, weil Händels eigene Angaben unklar sind. Eine ähnliche Verwirrung herrscht in *La Réjouissance*. Genauere Angaben hierzu finden sich in den Anmerkungen des Herausgebers (auf Englisch).

Erst mitten in *La Réjouissance* entschloss sich Händel dazu, Streicher hinzuzufügen, und er schrieb daraufhin am Anfang seiner Partitur „Violino I" usw. unter die ersten Takte der betreffenden Notensysteme. Am Rande der *Bourrée* ergänzte er „V. 1" und „V. 2" über den Bezeichnungen „H. 1" und „H. 2"[2]. Die Position dieser Angaben für Streicher zeigt, dass er sie nachträglich ergänzt hat, und ebenso ging er bei *La Paix* vor. In dem Menuett, das auf *La Réjouissance* folgt, stehen jedoch die Bezeichnungen für die Violinen genau vor dem Notensystem, sind also nicht nachträglich eingetragen worden, und das letzte Menuett hatte ursprünglich vier Notensysteme für Streicher. Die Verwirrung wird noch größer dadurch, dass die meisten Notensysteme für Streicher sowie die Angaben zur Verdoppelung der Stimmen in den späteren Stücken mit einem dünnen Strich durchgestrichen wurden. Diese Streichungen stammen wahrscheinlich von Händel, aber es gibt keine Belege dafür. Außerdem geht ein Strich durch die Worte „La seconda volta senza Hautb. e Bassons", die unter der *Bourrée* stehen, woraus an sich schon hervorgeht, dass in diesem Stück Streicher mitspielen. Wie ist es nun dazu gekommen, dass sich Händel anscheinend erst dazu entschloss, Streicher einzusetzen und sie dann aber doch nicht verwendete?

In der April-Ausgabe des *Gentleman's Magazine* wurde berichtet, dass hundert Musiker in Vauxhall mitgespielt hätten, und es ist behauptet worden, dies sei ein Beweis dafür, dass Händel seinen Willen durchgesetzt und Streicher verwendet hätte. Es ist jedoch unwahrscheinlich, dass er gegen den Wunsch des Königs gehandelt hat, und der Bericht über hundert oder mehr Musiker beruht wohl eher auf einer Schätzung als auf einer Zählung. Außerdem lässt sich das Ausstreichen am besten dadurch erklären, dass Händel verhindern wollte, die begrenzte Zeit seiner Kopisten für die Aufführung im Green Park mit dem Abschreiben von Streicherstimmen zu vergeuden, die nicht verwendet wurden. Bei der Komposition von *La Réjouissance* muss er darauf gekommen sein, dass er keine weiteren Aufführungen seiner Musik ohne Streicher erwarten konnte, weshalb er begann, sie mit einzubeziehen. Und um die Angaben nicht unkenntlich zu machen, da Walsh sie in seiner Ausgabe für weniger anspruchsvolle Aufführungen in geschlossenen Räumen veröffentlichen würde, machte er nur dünne Striche. Die erste dieser weiteren Aufführungen fand am 27. Mai im Londoner Foundling Hospital statt. Vielleicht sind auch die Angaben zur Verdoppelung der Stimmen in den früheren Stücken deshalb nicht ausgestrichen, weil er sie erst in seiner Partitur notierte, nachdem die Festlichkeiten im Green Park schon vorüber waren.

Außer diesen Nachträgen, die er mit großer Sorgfalt eintrug, ergänzte Händel später andere, nicht so sorgfältig geschriebene Angaben: „2 fois" [2 Mal] über der *Bourrée* und dem ersten Menuett sowie „the third time all together" [das dritte Mal alle zusammen] unter La *Réjouissance* hat er nur sehr flüchtig notiert. *GB-Lbl* RM20. g.7 enthält auch noch zwei Konzerte, deren Ähnlichkeit mit der *Feuerwerksmusik* mitunter übertrieben worden ist. In beiden erinnert die langsame Einleitung an die etwas längere Einleitung der Ouvertüre, aber ansonsten sind die Ähnlichkeiten sehr gering. Das Konzert in F ist mit Oboen, Fagotten, vier Hörnern und Streichern besetzt, beginnt mit zwei Hörnern allein und hat nur zwei Sätze. Das andere

---

[2] für „Hautboy" bzw. „Oboe"

Konzert steht in D, da Händel Trompeten und Pauken hinzufügen wollte, die damals nicht in F spielen konnten. In der Mitte ergänzte er eine Fuge:

Das Thema stammt aus der Ouvertüre der Feuerwerksmusik, T. 99–102. Die flüchtige Ähnlichkeit von T. 48 in der Ouvertüre (Holzbläser) und T. 1 in den letzten Sätzen der Konzerte (der Rhythmus ist hier jedoch nicht punktiert) scheint ein Zufall zu sein.

Gedruckte Ausgaben

Walsh verlor bei der Veröffentlichung der *Feuerwerksmusik* keine Zeit und gab sie „mit allen Stimmen, d. h. Hörnern, Trompeten, Pauken, Violinen, Oboen, Violoncello, Fagotten und einem Generalbass für Cembalo oder Orgel versehen" heraus. Eine Bratschenstimme war nicht dabei. Außerdem überging er das Notensystem für das „Basson I" in der Ouvertüre und erwähnte weder das Kontrafagott noch die kleine Trommel. Eine Stimme trägt die Bezeichnung „Hautboy & Violino I", eine andere „Hautboy & Violino II". „Hautboy III" spielt in den späteren Stücken zusammen mit „Hautboy II" und „Fagott, Kontrabass und Cello" sind beziffert. Somit sind die Stimmen der Streicher und Holzbläser durchweg übereinstimmend.

Ein Arrangement auf zwei Notensystemen für „Querflöte, Violine oder Cembalo" wurde ebenfalls herausgegeben und konnte zu Hause entweder allein am Klavier oder von einem Melodieinstrument mit Continuo-Begleitung (das untere System ist beziffert) gespielt werden. Walsh fügte am Ende sieben Märsche in D-Dur hinzu (darunter *See, the conquering Hero comes*, die Märsche aus *The Occasional Oratorio* und *Samson* sowie den Trauermarsch aus *Saul*) und ein Arrangement der Krönungshymne *Zadok the Priest*. Es gibt keine Belege dafür, dass diese zusätzliche Musik im Green Park gespielt wurde.

Anmerkungen des Herausgebers

AUT Händels Autograph der Partitur (*GB-Lbl* RM20.g.7)

PP Veröffentlichte Stimmen (Walsh, Anfang Juni 1749)

Hps Arrangement für Cembalo usw. (Walsh, Ende Juli 1749)

HG Händel-Gesellschaft, Band 47, herausgegeben von Friedrich Chrysander

Die vorliegende Eulenburg-Ausgabe basiert auf Händels Autograph der Partitur (AUT). Händels schriftliche Anmerkungen wurden nicht verändert, auch wenn sie beispielsweise am Ende in drei verschiedenen Sprachen notiert wurden. Ich habe die Angaben „Hautb." und „H. 1" in „Oboe" und „Ob. 1" abgeändert sowie „Principale im Sopranschlüssel" in „Tromba III im Violinschlüssel". In PP wurde die zuletzt genannte Änderung ebenfalls vorgenommen. Die „Principale" (Prinzipaltrompete) war eine Militärtrompete, die in der tiefen Lage unter dem Clarino spielte. Händel verwendete sie wie im *Dettinger Te Deum* fast nur für Arpeggionoten.

In der *Bourrée* notierte Händel „Viola colli Bassi", und die 4. Note in Takt 2 weist darauf hin, dass er „loco" (Oktavierung aufgehoben) meinte. Wenn das jedoch so wäre, müssten die Bratschen in Takt 5 auf der 2. Note eine Oktave nach oben springen. Sollten sie so bis zum Ende des Stückes weiterspielen? In *La Réjouissance* verstand Chrysander dagegen die Angabe „e Viola" in den Noten der „Tromba III" so, dass die Bratschen diese Stimme eine Oktave tiefer verdoppeln sollten. Kurz vor dem Wiederholungszeichen läuft dies jedoch auf Noten hinaus, die Händel unmöglich gemeint haben kann, obwohl sie in HG und vielen späteren Ausgaben auftauchen. Es ist nicht überraschend, dass Walsh nie eine Bratschenstimme veröffentlicht haben soll. Die Bratschenstimme, die mit dem Stimmenmaterial zur vorliegenden Partitur herausgegeben wurde, basiert auf Händels Angaben zur Verdoppelung der Stimmen, außer wenn sie untypisch für die Verwendung des Instruments im 18. Jahrhundert erscheinen. Zu Händels Zeiten arrangierten sich die Bratschisten selbst auf ähnliche Art und Weise.

Wie in der D-Dur-Suite der *Wassermusik*, gibt es auch hier keine dynamischen Angaben. Bei der Aufführung im Green Park haben vermutlich alle Instrumente im Fortissimo gespielt, wobei die dynamischen Gegensätze durch die Instrumentierung entstanden.

Eckige Klammern enthalten Ergänzungen des Herausgebers; vom Herausgeber hinzugefügte Bögen und Bindungen sind durch gestrichelte Linien gekennzeichnet.

Orchesterstimmen, die mit der vorliegenden Partitur übereinstimmen, sind beim Verlag erhältlich (Eulenburg Orchestral Series, EOS 1307). Die Partitur kann zum Dirigieren verwendet werden. Händels wesentliche Hinweise, die sich auf das zweite und dritte Mal beziehen, stehen in den Stimmen (auf Englisch), aber in der Praxis ist es unwahrscheinlich, dass Dirigenten ein Stück drei Mal mit Wiederholungen spielen lassen. (Ob Händel beim zweiten und dritten Mal Wiederholungen erwartet hat oder nicht, ist ungewiss.) Die übliche Lösung ist, seine das zweite Mal betreffenden Hinweise für die Wiederholungen beim ersten Mal zu befolgen und dann das Stück „all together" [alle zusammen]

ohne Wiederholungen zu spielen. Das ergibt für *La Réjouissance* folgende Anordnung:

{Erste Hälfte: Trompeten, Pauken (und Streicher?)

Erste Hälfte: nur von Holzbläsern und Hörnern wiederholt

{Zweite Hälfte: Trompeten, Pauken (und Streicher?)

Zweite Hälfte: nur von Holzbläsern und Hörnern wiederholt

Das ganze Stück „all together" bedeutet, dass alle zusammen das Stück ohne Wiederholungen spielen. Das gleiche gilt für das letzte Menuett.

Die von Händel angeführten Zahlen besagen, dass er die Stimme der ersten Oboe in der *Ouverture* verstärkt haben wollte. In den späteren Stücken wünschte er jedoch, dass jede Stimme von der gleichen Anzahl an Oboisten ausgeführt wird. Bei Aufführungen mit Streichern wird seine Absicht am besten dadurch berücksichtigt, indem man in der Ouvertüre sechs (3-2-1) oder vier (2-1-1) Oboisten spielen lässt. Eine Verdoppelung der Fagottstimmen ist ebenfalls sinnvoll. Im Green Park wurde sicherlich kein Cembalo verwendet, und auch heute ist dies nicht unbedingt notwendig.

Roger Fiske
Übersetzung: Stefan de Haan

PRÉFACE

La guerre de Succession d'Autriche prit officiellement fin à la signature du traité de paix d'Aix-la Chapelle, le 7 octobre 1748. Les fêtes entourant cet évènement, repoussées afin de profiter d'un temps plus clément, furent organisées à Londres le 27 avril 1749. Au cours de l'hiver précédent fut édifié dans Green Park un pavillon au style recherché d'où les membres de la famille royale et d'autres notables pourraient assister aux feux d'artifice et entendre la musique de Haendel. On engagea pour l'occasion des maîtres artificiers italiens. Le 28 mars, le Duke of Monmouth écrivit à l'Administrateur des Feux d'artifice de Sa Majesté :

Hendel [sic] propose maintenant d'utiliser 12 trompettes et 12 cors. Il devait d'abord y avoir seize de chaque et je me souviens en avoir informé le roi qui, à cette époque, n'était pas d'accord pour qu'il y ait de la musique. Mais, quand je lui décrivis l'abondante musique martiale qui devait être jouée, il fut satisfait et dit qu'il espérait qu'il n'y aurait pas de violons. Hendel propose maintenant de réduire le nombre de trompettes, etc., et de faire appel à des violons. Je ne doute pas que quand le roi l'apprendra, il sera fort mécontent. Si ce concert devait se conformer au plaisir du roi, il ne devrait pas comporter d'autres instruments que des instruments militaires.[1]

Jonathan Tyers, propriétaire de Vauxhall Gardens, offrit de prêter pour l'occasion « toutes ses lanternes, lampes, etc. pour la valeur de sept cents livres », ainsi que trente de ses hommes pour les installer à condition de faire répéter la musique de Haendel à Vauxhall. Haendel s'opposa à cette idée mais ne fut pas écouté, car l'économie réalisée était irrésistible. A ce moment-là, il avait réduit sa formation à 9 trompettes et 9 cors, accompagnés de 24 hautbois, 12 bassons, un contrebasson et peut-être un serpent, 3 paires de timbales et 2 (?) caisses claires – en tout au moins 60 musiciens. Il inscrivit ces chiffres sur sa partition pour s'assu-

[1] Cité in : Otto Erich Deutsch, *Handel, a Documentary Biography*, Londres, 1955, p.661

rer que les parties séparées fussent copiées en nombre suffisant.

La répétition à Vauxhall Gardens eut lieu le 21 avril à 11 heures et, d'après le *Gentleman's Magazine*, 12 000 personnes s'acquittèrent d'une demi-couronne pour entrer dans les jardins. « Un si grand évènement créa un tel encombrement de London Bridge qu'aucune voiture ne put passer pendant trois heures », bien que Westminster Bridge, plus proche, ait été aussi ouvert. A Green Park, la musique commença peu après six heures et fut suivie des feux d'artifice. Il n'est pas prouvé que musique et feux d'artifice aient été simultanés. A l'embrasement d'une partie du pavillon, « le Chevalier Servandoni qui avait conçu ce bâtiment, tira son épée et affronta […] l'Administrateur de l'Ordonnance et des Feux d'artifice, il fut désarmé et placé en garde à vue, mais relâché le lendemain après s'être excusé. »

Le manuscrit autographe de Haendel

La partition autographe de Haendel, conservée à la British Library, Royal Music Collection (*GB-Lbl* RM20.g.7), constitue l'unique source importante. Elle se présente de façon très confuse car, après son exécution à Green Park (ou peut-être juste avant), Haendel y ajouta des parties de cordes, généralement par simple doublure des instruments à vent. Il inséra également, à la même occasion, des instructions concernant la reprise de certaines pièces avec une instrumentation différente, mais il est difficile de dire si ces recommandations s'appliquent aux exécutions avec ou sans cordes. La comparaison d'éditions antérieures du *Minuet* final donnera une idée des embûches rencontrées pour l'établissement d'un *Urtext* : Chrysander disposa le menuet sur dix portées, les Corno 1 et Corno 2 doublant la Tromba 1, or l'édition Eulenburg précédente le dispose sur onze portées, le Corno 1 doublant la Tromba 1. Ces deux partitions comportent les instructions de reprise de

Haendel, mais aucune n'indique clairement quels instruments doivent jouer la première fois, car Haendel lui-même ne le définit pas nettement. On trouve une semblable imprécision dans *La Réjouissance*. (Voir l'appareil critique en anglais pour les détails complets.)

Haendel avait composé la moitié de *La Réjouissance* quand il pensa à ajouter des cordes à son instrumentation. Il inscrivit au début de sa partition « *e Violino I, etc.* » sous les premières mesures des portées correspondantes et ajouta « V.1 » et « V.2 » dans la marge de la *Bourrée* au-dessus des H.1 et H.2 [2] placés au centre de la page. L'alignement prouve que ces indications de cordes sont des additions plus tardives, ce qui est également le cas dans *La Paix*. Dans le *Minuet* qui suit *La Réjouissance*, les indications de violon sont cependant exactement placées face aux portées et non ajoutées ensuite et la partition du *Minuet* final comportait à l'origine quatre portées de cordes. Pour augmenter la confusion, la plupart des portées de cordes et des indications de doublure des dernières pièces ont été légèrement rayées, probablement, mais ce n'est pas sûr, par Haendel lui-même. Une ligne barre également les mots « *La seconda volta senza Hautb. e Bassons* » qui portent en eux l'implication de la présence de cordes dans cette pièce. Pourquoi Haendel aurait-il décidé de recourir à des cordes, puis de ne pas les employer ?

Le *Gentleman's Magazine* du mois d'avril rapportant la présence de cent instrumentistes, on peut conclure d'après ce nombre que Haendel avait imposé ses vues sur le recours aux cordes, mais il semble improbable qu'il se soit opposé aux désirs du roi et cette description d'un orchestre de cent musiciens s'apparente plus à une estimation qu'à un comptage des instrumentistes. De plus, l'explication la plus convaincante des mesures barrées réside sans doute dans le fait que Haendel ne voulut pas perdre le temps limité de ses copistes de Green Park sur des parties de cordes qui n'étaient pas souhaitées. En composant *La Réjouissance*, Haendel réalisa que cette musique ne serait plus exécutée

si elle ne comportait pas de parties de cordes et il commença donc à les y inclure. Il raya ces parties légèrement de façon à ne pas dissimuler ce que Walsh allait ensuite publier pour des exécutions dans des salles plus modestes, dont la première prit place au Foundling Hospital, à Londres, le 27 mai. Peut-être les indications de doublure des pièces précédentes ne furent-elles pas barrées parce que Haendel ne les ajouta qu'après la fin des festivités de Green Park.

A côté des ajouts qu'il nota soigneusement, Haendel en inscrivit d'autres plus négligemment : « 2 fois » au-dessus de la *Bourrée* et du premier *Minuet* et « la troisième fois tous ensemble » en dessous de *La Réjouissance* furent assurément griffonnés à la hâte. Cet autographe (*GB-Lbl* RM20.g.7) comprend aussi deux concertos dont la ressemblance avec *Fireworks Music* a parfois été exagérée. La lente introduction de chacun d'eux est très proche de celle plus longue de l'Ouverture, mais leurs autres points communs sont peu significatifs. Le Concerto en *fa*, est instrumenté pour hautbois, bassons, 4 cors et cordes, s'ouvre avec deux cors seuls et ne comporte que deux mouvements. L'autre concerto est en *ré* car Haendel voulait y ajouter des trompettes et des timbales qui ne pouvaient alors pas jouer en *fa*. Il intercala également une fugue entre les deux :

Ce sujet est tiré des mesures 99 à 102 de l'ouverture de *Fireworks Music*. La brève parenté entre la mesure 48 de l'Ouverture (par les bois) et la mesure 1 du final du concerto (sans rythme pointé) est certainement le fruit d'une coïncidence.

Éditions publiées

Walsh publia rapidement *Fireworks Music* « dans toutes ses parties, avec cors, trompettes, timbales,

---

[2] Pour « Hautboy »

violons, hautbois, violoncelle et bassons ; avec une basse continue pour le clavecin ou l'orgue ». Il n'y incorpora pas de partie d'alto, ignora également la portée de « Basson I » de l'Ouverture et ne mentionna ni contrebasson, ni caisse claire. Une partie est intitulée « Hautboy & Violino I », un autre « Hautbois & Violino II », le Hautboy III double le Hautboy II dans les dernières pièces et la partie de « Basson e C.Basso e Violoncello » est chiffrée. Les parties de cordes et de bois sont donc ainsi les mêmes d'un bout à l'autre.

Un arrangement réduit sur deux portées pour « Flûte allemande, Violon ou Clavecin » parut également en vue d'exécutions au clavier seul ou par un instrument mélodique accompagné d'une basse continue (la portée inférieure est chiffrée). Walsh fit suivre cet arrangement de sept marches en ré majeur (parmi lesquelles *See, the conquering Hero comes*, les marches de *Occasional Oratorio* et de *Samson*, ainsi que la marche funèbre de *Saul*) et d'un arrangement de l'hymne du Couronnement *Zadok the Priest*, mais rien ne prouve que ces pièces furent jouées à Green Park.

Appareil critique

AUT : manuscrit autographe de Haendel (British Library, *GB-Lbl* RM20.g.7)
PP : parties publiées (*published parts*) (Walsh, début juin 1749)
Hps : arrangement pour clavecin (*harpsichord*), etc. (publié par Walsh, fin juillet 1749)
HG : *Händelgesellschaft*, vol. 47, édition de Friedrich Chrysander

Cette édition Eulenburg se fonde sur la source AUT. Les instructions formulées par Haendel sont inchangées, même celles qui, comme à la fin, apparaissent en trois langues différentes. J'ai remplacé les termes *Hautb.* et *H.1* par *Oboe* et *Ob.1* (hautbois et htb.1), ainsi que *Principale in the soprano clef* par *Tromba in the treble clef* (Trompette en clef de *sol*). La source PP effectua aussi ce dernier changement. Le *Principale* désignait la trompette militaire jouant dans le registre grave, en opposition au *Clarino* jouant dans le registre aigu. De même que dans le *Te*

Deum de Dettingen, Haendel réserva presqu' exclusivement son usage aux arpèges.

Dans la *Bourrée*, Haendel écrivit « *Viola colli Bassi* », or la 4e note de la mesure 2 fait penser qu'il voulait dire *loco* mais, dans ce cas, les altos doivent sauter une octave à partir de la 2e note de la mesure 5. Doivent-ils maintenir cette position jusqu'à la fin de la pièce ? Dans *La Réjouissance*, Chrysander vit « *e Viola* » contre la portée de Tromba III et décida que les altos devaient doubler à l'octave inférieure, mais, en ce cas, Haendel n'a sûrement pas envisagé les notes précédant immédiatement les points de reprise bien qu'elles figurent dans la source HG et dans de nombreuses édition ultérieures. Il n'est pas surprenant que Walsh n'ait jamais publié de partie d'alto. La partie d'alto réalisée dans le matériel fondé sur cette édition se conforme aux indications de doublure fournies par Haendel sauf aux endroits où celle-ci dépasse les limites de l'instrument du XVIIIe siècle. Du temps de Haendel, les altistes ajustaient ainsi leur partie de leur propre initiative.

De même que dans la Suite en ré majeur de *Water Music*, aucune indication de nuances n'apparaît sur cette partition. A Green Park, tous les instruments ont dû jouer *fortissimo*, les contrastes dynamiques provenant de l'orchestration.

Indications ajoutées à l'édition. Les additions éditoriales sont placées entre crochets. Les liaisons de phrasé ou les liaisons de notes ajoutées à l'édition figurent en pointillé.

Les parties séparées instrumentales correspondant à cette édition sont disponibles auprès de l'éditeur (Eulenburg Orchestral Series, EOS 1307). Cette partition peut être utilisée pour la direction. L'essentiel des instructions de deuxième et troisième fois de Haendel figurent (en anglais) dans les parties séparées. Dans la pratique, toutefois, aucun chef d'orchestre ne fera jouer une pièce trois fois avec ses reprises (la question demeure de savoir si Haendel attendait les reprises lors des deuxième et troisième fois). La solution généralement adoptée est d'appliquer les recommandations pour la deuxième fois aux reprises de la première fois et de jouer la pièce « *all together* », c'est-à-dire sans reprises. Ainsi de l'exécution de *La Réjouissance* :

{ 1ère moitié : trompettes, timbales (et cordes ?)
1ère moitié : reprise par les seuls bois et cors
{ 2ème moitié : trompettes, timbales (et cordes ?)
2ème moitié : reprise par les seuls bois et cors

La pièce « *all together* » (d'une traite) sans reprises. La démarche sera la même dans le *Minuet* final.

Les effectifs de Haendel montrent qu'il souhaitait faire ressortir la partie de Hautbois 1 dans l'Ouverture, mais que dans les pièces suivantes, il voulait le même nombre de hautboïstes pour chaque partie. Lors des exécutions avec cordes, ses intentions seront respectées au mieux avec six hautboïstes (3–2–1 dans l'Ouverture) ou quatre (2–1–1 dans l'Ouverture). Les parties de basson seront doublées. Les chiffrages surmontant la ligne de basse des sources PP et Hps ne figurent pas dans cette partition ni dans la source AUT. Il ne pouvait pas y avoir de clavecin à Green Park, il n'y en a donc aucune nécessité aujourd'hui.

Roger Fiske
Traduction : Agnès Ausseur

MUSICK FOR THE ROYAL FIREWORKS

George Frideric Handel
(1685–1759)
HWV 351

I. Ouverture

[Largo]

Edited by Roger Fiske
© 2010 Ernst Eulenburg Ltd, London
and Ernst Eulenburg & Co GmbH, Mainz

4

6

18

20

[*Fine*]

34

36

Lentement

Da capo $\frac{3}{4}$ fine al segno ⌢

[bb47–117]

40

II. Bourrée 2 fois

Oboe 1 *for 12*
e Violino I

Oboe 2 *for 12*
e Violino II

Viola colli Bassi

Bassons tutti
[Violoncelli e Bassi]

Ob. 1
Vl. I

Ob. 2
Vl. II

Bsn., Vc.
Bassi

Ob. 1
Vl. I

Ob. 2
Vl. II

Bsn., Vc.
Bassi

La seconda volta senza Hautb. e Bassons

III. La Paix

Largo alla Siciliana

Corno 1
for 3 persons

Corno 2
for 3 persons

Corno 3
for 3 persons

Oboe 1
for 12 persons
e Violino I

Oboe 2
for 12 persons
e Violino II

Viola colli Bassi

Bassons
Vc. e Cb.

1

Cor. 2

3

Ob. 1
(Vl. I)

Ob. 2
(Vl. II)

Bsn.
Vc. e Cb.

44

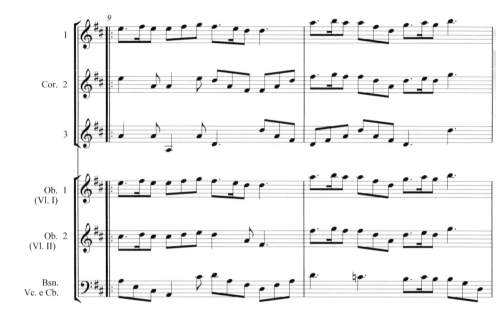

IV. La Réjouissance

Allegro

Tromba 1
for 3
(Corno 1)

Tromba 2
for 3
(Corno 2)

Tromba 3
for 3
(Corno 3)

Timpani

Violino I
(Oboe 1)

Violino II
(Oboe 2)

Viola

Violoncello
e Contra Bassi
(Bassons)

With the Side Drum

Tr.
(Cor.) 1

2

3

Timp.

Ob. 1
(Vl. I)

Ob. 2
(Vl. II)

Vla.

Vc. e Cb.
(Bsns.)

48

The second time *by the French Horns and Hautbois and Bassons without Trumpets and Kettle Drums*

The third time *all together*

49

V. Menuet [I] 2 fois

Menuet [II]

51

La seconda volta *colli* Corni da Caccia, Hautbois et Bassons
La terza volta *tutti insieme and the Side Drums*